US Immigration Exam Study Guide in English and Spanish

Mike Swedenberg

Translation by Edith DeLeon
Se estudia para convertirse en un ciudadano de los Estados Unidos
Source: U.S. Citizenship and Immigration Services
Fuente: Servicios de la ciudadanía y de la inmigración de Estados Unidos

Contact me at: Mike@Swedenberg.com

Twitter: @USAcitizenship

Study Guide
100 Sample Questions and Answers for the US Immigration Test
in Spanish and English
A unique product, professionally developed and annotated
Updated 2023. / . Actualización 2023

The U.S. Citizenship Services (USCIS) administers a verbal test to all immigrants applying for citizenship. This study guide tutors Spanish speaking immigrants for the USCIS verbal citizenship test in English and Spanish. The questions have been selected from questions used on past exams by the USCIS.

Studying these questions does not guarantee obtaining citizenship to the United States.

Guía de estudio

100 preguntas y respuestas para el nuevo examen de USCIS en inglés y español para el 2011

Un producto único, desarrollado y registrado profesionalmente que será un éxito inmediato en el mercado hispánico.

Los inmigrantes de habla hispana de los profesores particulares para la ciudadanía verbal de USCIS prueban en inglés y español.

Los servicios de la ciudadanía de ESTADOS UNIDOS (USCIS) administran una prueba verbal a todos los inmigrantes que solicitan ciudadanía.

La lista siguiente de 100 preguntas se ha seleccionado de las preguntas usadas encendido más allá de exámenes.

Estudiar estas preguntas no garantiza la obtención de ciudadanía

a los Estados Unidos.

TRANSLATOR INTRODUCTION

Hello, my name is Edith DeLeon. I was born in Quito, Ecuador. My parents are Ecuadorians and I'm very proud to be Ecuadorian-American.

I grew up with both cultures. I had the opportunity to study at a college and become a citizen of the United States. I have prospered and I own my home and business in New York and North Carolina. I also work for a company of Certified Public Accountants in the department of information technology for 23 years.

I have a beautiful family, husband and 2 daughters, who also reap the benefits of being born and growing up in the U.S.

One problem with the citizenship test is access to the questions and answers to study. Professor Domiciliary makes this task easier and inexpensive. The professor asked me to help create this new study guide just for you.

Now you have a sample of the questions in Spanish and English.

Thank you very much.
Edith

Hola, mi nombre es Edith DeLeon- nací en Quito, Ecuador. Mis padres son Ecuatorianos.

Yo estoy muy orgullosa de ser Ecuatoriana-Americana, crecí con las dos culturas. Tuve la oportunidad de estudiar en un Colegio y hacerme una ciudadana própera de los E.U.Actualmente vivo y soy propietaria de mi casa y negocios en New York y North Carolina. Tambien trabajo en una Companía de Contadores, en el departamento de tecnologia e información por 23 años.

Tengo una hermosa familia, esposo y 2 hijas, quienes tambien cosechan los beneficios de nacer y crecer en los E.U.

Uno de los problemas es cogar la prueba de la ciudadania,y tener acceso a las preguntas y respuestas para estudiar. El profesor Domiciliario,hace esta tarea mas facil y muy económica. El Profesor me pidió ayuda para crear este nuevo guía de estudio justo para Usted.

Ahora Ud tiene una muestra de las preguntas en Espanól e Ingles.

Muchas Gracias
Edith

ACKNOWLEDGMENTS

We gratefully acknowledge The U.S. Citizenship Services (USCIS) for their cooperation and Mrs. Edith Deleon for her hard work in the translation.

Languages available
Spanish, Polish, French, Portuguese, Russian, Vietnamese, Tagalog,
Korean and an English only version.
In Print and eBooks at Amazon.com

CONTENTS

"I pledge allegiance to the flag of the United States of America, and to the republic for which it stands, one nation under God, indivisible, with liberty and justice for all."

INTRODUCTION

The 100 sample questions and answers for the US Immigration test are listed below. The test is an oral exam in which the USCIS Officer will ask the applicant up to 10 of the 100 questions. An applicant must answer six out of ten questions correctly to pass the civics portion of the test.

On the naturalization test, some answers may change because of elections or appointments. As you study for the test, make sure that you know the most current members of Congress, Senate, Speaker of the House and Governor of your state and district.

This publication is the only study guide that provides this information and updates it throughout the year.

We also provide you with the Sample Written Questions which all applicants must know how to write in English.

INTRODUCCIÓN

Las 100 preguntas de muestra y sus respuestas para la prueba de Inmigración de EEUU, están listadas abajo. La prueba es un examen oral en el que el Oficial de USCIS le preguntará hasta 10 de las 100 preguntas. Usted debe responder seis de diez preguntas correctamente para pasar la parte de civismo de la prueba. En la prueba de nacionalización, algunas respuestas podrían cambiar debido a las elecciones y nombramientos. A medida que usted estudie para la prueba, asegúrese de que usted conoce la mayoría de miembros actuales del congreso, senado, vocero de la cámara y el gobernador de su estado y distrito.

Esta publicación es la única guía de estudio que provee esta información y la actualiza a lo largo del año. También le proveemos con la muestra de preguntas escritas, que todos los aplicantes deben conocer como escribir en Ingles.

Advice

from the Immigration Law offices of

KURCZABA LAW OFFICES P.C.

6219 N. Milwaukee - Chicago, IL 60646

10661 S. Roberts Rd., Palos Hills, IL 60465

(773) 774-0000

www.kurczabalaw.com

BECOMING A CITIZEN

The day of your interview, you will be asked to appear at a specific date and time at the

Immigration Office. For interviews in Chicago, our interview will take place at:

101 W. Ida B. Wells (formerly Congress Parkway), 3rd Floor

Chicago

Bring to the interview:

Interview notice

Passports – all your passports, current and expired

Permanent Resident Card (green card)

Driver's License/ ID

Income Tax Returns – bring your last 5 years of tax returns (may be asked)

Alimony/Child Support – (if required to pay) – bring proof of payment Check In:

Arrive 30 minutes before your scheduled interview

Check in with the receptionist (in Chicago - on the 3rd floor) – they will give you a number

You will be called by number

Interview:

When called, you will enter the officer's room, and:

Oath – swear that you will tell the truth.

Fingerprint /identification– the officer will take your photograph (using a digital camera) and ask you to place your left and right index finger on a little black box on their desk.

Administer the following test

1.TEST

Questions 100 possible Questions – as listed in this book.

You will be given 10 questions - 2 from each section,

You must have 6 correct. As soon as you have 6 correct – you pass and the question portion of the test ends.

Reading- you will be asked to read a question out loud to the officer (usually shown on an iPad)

Writing – you will be asked to write a sentence on the same iPad which is dictated to you. (in Chicago – this is often the answer to the question you just read)

2.APPLICATION

You will be asked questions from the Citizenship Application (form N400).

Biographical information

Name (your full name – first, middle last) as shown on your birth certificate

Any other names used – including your maiden (before marriage) name

Address, telephone,

Your marital status

Spouse's name, date of birth, date of marriage, immigration status (if out of status – you may state this, you may also state that you are applying for permanent residency for them). If your spouse is a US Citizen already, you may bring a copy of their Naturalization Certificate

Children – their names, dates of birth, locations of birth, current address (often city is sufficient)

Details on employment, residency

Travel History – when is the last time you left the United States? Sometimes officers will ask you have you left the United States since filing your N-400 application? OR Have you ever been outside of the United States for 180 days or longer? You may check your travel history on the Customs and Border Protection Website at: https://i94.cbp.dhs.gov/I94/#/home

If you have been outside of the United States for longer than 180 days at any one time, be prepared to provide detailed information as to why you stayed outside of the country for so long. If for education reasons – provide proof of attending school, for job reasons – bring a letter from your employer, because of illness – bring proof of your seeking medical attention.

It is up to the Immigration Officer to determine whether your permanent place of residence is in the United States, and there was good reason for you to have to remain outside of the country for > 6 months. Officers will look to the exact reasons for your staying longer outside the country.

In the past 5 years, you must have spent at least > ½ of that time in the United States. This means out of 1,825 days; you must have spent > 913 days in the United States. If you have not – you do not qualify for naturalization.

Did you ever serve in the military? When? What branch?

How you received permanent residency?

If you obtained permanent residency through a spouse – are you still married to that spouse? Bring proof with you including joint filed tax returns, bank account statements, insurance statements, proof of residency. If you are divorced – bring your divorce decree (issued by a court) and be ready to explain why you were divorced.

If you obtained permanent residency through an employer – be prepared to give information about your sponsoring employer, the name of the owner, address and telephone of the company, and the occupation you were sponsored in for permanent residency. The officer may also ask if you had experience in that occupation before being sponsored, and where you were working to gain that experience.

Your eligibility for citizenship – most asked questions – see later questions for a full listing.

Did you ever claim to be a US Citizen?

The immigration service has been adopting a strict

approach to this question. If you have ever stated that you were a citizen, you can expect to be denied and the Immigration Service to start proceedings against you to lose your permanent residence.

Did you ever vote or register to vote in an American election?

Did you ever discriminate against anyone?

Did you ever lie to immigration/ use false documents?

Do you owe any taxes?

Did you ever file taxes as a nonresident (after receiving your permanent residency)?

Do you have a title of nobility?

Were you ever a member of the military?

If so – was it mandatory? When did you serve? What was your title/rank?

Do you have any weapons training?

If so – what kind of weapons?

Are you a member of a terrorist or socialist organization?

If a male, did you live in the US between ages 18-26? Did you register for Selective Service?

Be prepared to provide proof of the registration which you can obtain by checking the Selective Service

Administration at
https://www.sss.gov/Home/Verification

Citizenship Issues

Are you ready to take the oath of allegiance?

Did you read and understand the oath? (copy in this book)

If the law requires, are you ready to sign up to the military and defend the United States?

If the law requires, are you ready to assist the government in a civilian capacity in a time of national emergency?

OATH

You will be asked if you are ready to take the Oath of Citizenship. You should be familiar with what the oath says, but do not have to memorize it. The oath generally says that you will be loyal to the United States and defend this country.

I hereby declare, on oath, that I absolutely and entirely renounce and abjure all allegiance and fidelity to any foreign prince, potentate, state, or sovereignty, of whom or which I have heretofore been a subject or citizen; that I will support and defend the Constitution and laws of the

United States of America against all enemies, foreign and domestic; that I will bear true faith and allegiance to the same; that I will bear arms on behalf of the United States when required by the law; that I will perform noncombatant service in the Armed Forces of the United States when required by the law; that I will perform work of national importance under civilian direction when required by the law; and that I take this obligation freely, without any mental reservation or purpose of evasion; so help me God."

TEST

1. 10 Questions (6 correct)

2. Read a Question Out Loud

3. Write a Sentence

Three Tests for Citizenship

Most applicants for citizenship or naturalization as it is called, are subject to THREE different "tests" when applying. It is important that an individual understand that in applying for Citizenship their entire immigration history is being reviewed and an Immigration Officer is making a determination not only over whether an applicant passes a test, but moreover, is reviewing the applicant's entire immigration history.

The Citizenship process should be looked upon as a complex, detailed demanding process, not just the completion of a form and passing of a simple civics test. This is not a process that should be taken lightly.

Often persons get "free" help with benevolent charities completing applications during large scale meetings. However, an applicant can face severe consequences including the loss of their permanent residency and even removal from the United States if certain matters come to the attention of an Immigration Officer reviewing your application.

First and foremost are persons who have ever been arrested, detained, or even stopped by a Police Officer. These individuals should ensure they seek the assistance of an attorney to review their criminal record before proceeding with the filing of an application for Citizenship.

Each Applicant for Citizenship undergoes three tests:

1. Test of Civics/History/Government, Reading & Writing

a. Civics/history test of 10 questions chosen out of a possible 100

b. Reading – applicants will be asked to read out loud a sample sentence from a fixed set of possible sentences

c. Writing – applicants will be asked to write a sentence dictated by an Immigration Officer.

2. Ability to Communicate in English

a. The Immigration Officer will review your application with you. Traditionally, this takes place after you pass your test. This portion can be difficult for those that do not speak English well.

b. The Immigration Officer will speak to you in English to determine if you generally can communicate.

3. Eligibility –a review of an Applicant's personal history

a. The Immigration Officer will review your entire immigration file and determine if you have the proper character to become a citizen. The Officer will literally have before them your entire immigration history including every form and piece of paper that you submitted to the Immigration Service. This includes your applications for immigration benefits before permanent residency.

i. The Officer will review how you obtained your green card or permanent residency.

1. If you received your permanent residency through marriage to a US Citizen, then the Immigration Officer will ask questions about your marriage. The Officer can question whether the marriage was legitimate.

2. If you received your permanent residency through a family member – the Immigration Officer will review your original application to make sure there were no improprieties when you applied.

3. If you received your permanent residency through an employer – the Immigration Officer can ask you questions about the employer and the employment relationship.

ii. The Officer will review your criminal background – checking if you were ever arrested/detained/stopped by a Police Officer at home or abroad.

1. For the Immigration Service- to be stopped, arrested, or detained means precisely that – any time a Police agency would take your fingerprints

a. Regardless of the eventual outcome of the case – or what you think it means to be arrested – you will be expected to admit to all times that you were arrested/stopped or detained by a Police agency.

i. Sometimes applicants believe that an arrest means serving time in jail. But the Immigration Service has a much broader interpretation – including anytime that a Police agency would take your fingerprints and record the information.

ii. The Immigration Service obtains criminal background information on individuals primarily from the FBI. The FBI retains this information forever, regardless of expungements, or local agencies clearing of a criminal history.

AMERICAN GOVERNMENT
GOBIERNO AMERICANO

I. Principles of American Democracy / Principios de democracia americana

1. What is the supreme law of the land?

The Constitution

¿Cuál es la legislación nacional suprema?

La constitución

2. What does the Constitution do?

Sets up the government

Defines the government

Protects basic rights of Americans

¿Qué hace la constitución?

Establece el gobierno

Define un gobierno

Protege derechos fundamentales de americanos

3. The idea of self-government is in the first three words of the Constitution. What are these words?

We the People

La idea del gobierno autónomo está en las primeras tres palabras de la constitución. ¿Cuáles son estas palabras?

Nosotros la gente

4. What is an amendment?

A change to the Constitution.

An addition to the Constitution.

¿Cuál es una enmienda?

un cambio a la constitución.

una adición a la constitución.

5. What do we call the first ten amendments to the Constitution?

The Bill of Rights

¿Qué llamamos las primeras diez enmiendas a la constitución?

La Declaración de Derechos

6. What is one right or freedom from the First Amendment? (You need to know one answer)

Speech

Religion

Assembly

Press

Petition the government

¿Cuál es un derecho o libertad de la Primera Enmienda? *(Hay tres respuestas correctas, necesita saber uno)

Discurso

Religion

Asamblea

Prensa

Peticion al gobierno

7. How many amendments does the Constitution have?

Twenty-seven (27)

¿Cuántas enmiendas la constitución tiene?

Veintisiete (27)

8. What did the Declaration of Independence do?

Announced our independence (from Great Britain)

Declared our independence (from Great Britain)

Said that the United States is free (from Great Britain)

¿Qué hizo la Declaración de Independencia?

Anunció nuestra independencia (de Gran Bretaña)

Declaró nuestra independencia (de Gran Bretaña)

Declaro que los Estados Unidos están libres (de Gran Bretaña)

9. What are two rights in the Declaration of Independence?

Life

Liberty

Pursuit of Happiness

¿Cuáles son dos derechos en la Declaración de Independencia?

Vida

Libertad

Búsqueda de la felicidad

10. What is freedom of religion?

You can practice any religion, or not practice a religion.

¿Cuál es la libertad de religión?

Puedes practicar cualquier religión, o no practicar una religión.

11. What is the economic system in the United States?*

capitalist economy

market economy

¿Cuál es el sistema económico en los Estados Unidos? *

economía capitalista

economía de mercado

12. What is the "rule of law"?

Everyone must follow the law

Leaders must obey the law.

Government must obey the law.

No one is above the law

Cuáles son las " ¿reglas de las leyes "?

Cada uno debe seguir la ley.

Los líderes deben obedecer la ley.

El gobierno debe obedecer la ley.

Nadie está sobre la ley.

System of Government / Sistema de gobierno

13. Name one branch or part of the government.*

Congress

Legislative

President

Executive

The courts

Judicial

Nombre una rama o porción del govierno.*

Congreso

Legislativo

Presidente

Ejecutivo

Las cortes

Judicial

14. What stops one branch of government from becoming too powerful?

Checks and balances

Separation of powers

Qué le detine a una rama de gobierno para llegar hacer demasiado poderoso?

Controles y equilibrios

Separación de poderes

15. Who is in charge of the executive branch?

The President

¿Quién está a cargo del Poder Ejecutivo?

el presidente

16. Who makes federal laws?

Congress

Senate and House (of Representatives)

(U.S. or national) legislature

¿Quién hace las leyes federales?

Congreso

Senado (de representantes)

(los E.E.U.U. o nacional) legislatura

17. What are the two parts of the U.S. Congress?*

The Senate and House (of Representatives)

¿Cuáles son las dos partes del congreso de los E.E.U.U.? *

el Senado y la casa de representantes

18. How many U.S. Senators are there?

One hundred (100)

¿Cuántos senadores de los E.E.U.U. hay?

Cien (100)

19. We elect a U.S. Senator for how many years?

Six (6)

¿Elegimos a senador de los E.E.U.U. por cuántos años?

Seis (6)

20. Who is one of your state's U.S. Senators?*

See List of Representatives in back of book and write the answer here:____

* If you are 65 years old or older and have been a legal permanent resident of the United States for 20 or more years, you may study just the questions that have been marked with an asterisk.

> * Si eres 65 años o más y has sido un residente permanente legal de los Estados Unidos por 20 o más años, puedes estudiar apenas las preguntas que se han marcado con un asterisco.

21. The House of Representatives has how many voting members?

> Four hundred thirty-five (435)

> ¿Cuantos miembros votantes tiene La cámara de representantes?

> Cuatrocientos treinta y cinco (435)

22. We elect a U.S. Representative for how many years?

> Two (2)

> ¿Elegimos un representante de los E.E.U.U. por cuántos años?

> Dos (2)

23. Name your U.S. Representative. (Congressman or Congresswomen)

> Answers will vary. [Residents of territories with nonvoting Delegates or resident Commissioners may provide the name of that Delegate or Commissioner. Also acceptable is any statement that the territory has no (voting) Representatives in Congress.]

Nombre tu representante de los E.E.U.U.

Las respuestas variarán. [Los residentes de territorios con los delegados no electorales o los comisionados residentes pueden proporcionar el nombre de ese delegado o comisionado. También aceptable es cualquier declaración que el territorio no tiene ningun(a) representante (de votación) en congreso.]

See List of Representatives in back of book and write the answer here:____

24. Who does a U.S. Senator represent?

All people of the state

¿Quién representa un senador de los E.E.U.U.?

Toda la gente del estado

25. Why do some states have more Representatives than other states?

There are three correct answers. You need to know one answer.

Because of the state's population

Because they have more people

Because some states have more people

¿Por qué algunos estados tienen más representantes que otros estados?

Hay tres respuestas correctas, necesita saber uno.

Debido a la población del estado

Porque tienen más gente

Porque algunos estados tienen más gente

26. We elect a President for how many years?

Four (4)

¿Elegimos a presidente por cuántos años?

Cuatro (4)

27. In what month do we vote for President?*

November

¿En qué mes votamos por un presidente? *

Noviembre

28. What is the name of the President of the United States now?*

President Joseph Biden

¿Cuál es el nombre del Presidente de los Estados Unidos ahora? *

29. What is the name of the Vice President of the United States now?

Vice President Elect Michael R. Pence

¿Cuál es el nombre del vice presidente de los Estados Unidos ahora?

30. If the President can no longer serve, who becomes President?

The Vice President

¿Si el presidente no puede servir más, quien hace de presidente?

El vice presidente

31. If both the President and the Vice President can no longer serve, who becomes President?

The Speaker of the House

¿Si el presidente y el vice presidente no pueden servir más, quien hace de presidente?

El orador de la casa

32. Who is the Commander in Chief of the military?

The President

¿Quién es el comandante y jefe de los militares?

El presidente

33. Who signs bills to become laws?

The President

¿Quién firma propuestas para convertirse en leyes?

El presidente

34. Who vetoes bills?

The President

¿Quién veta propuestas?

El presidente

35. What does the President's Cabinet do?

Advises the President

¿Qué hace el Gabinete del presidente?

Aconseja al presidente

36. What are two Cabinet-level positions?

Secretary of State

Secretary of Labor

Cuáles son dos niveles de posiciones del Cabinete?

El secretario(a) de Estado

El secretario(a) del trabajo

37. What does the judicial branch do?

Reviews laws

Explains laws

Resolves disputes (disagreements)

decides if a law goes against the Constitution

¿Que hace la rama judicial?

Revisar leyes

Explica leyes

Resulven los desacuerdos

Decide si una ley va contra la constitución

38. What is the highest court in the United States?

The Supreme Court

¿Cuál es el tribunal más superior de los Estados Unidos?

El Tribunal Supremo

39. How many justices are on the Supreme Court?

Nine (9)

¿Cuántos jueces hay en el Tribunal Supremo?

Nueve (9)

40. Who is the Chief Justice of the United States?

John G. Roberts, Jr.

¿Quién es el principal jues de los Estados Unidos?

John G. Roberts, Jr.

41. Under our Constitution, some powers belong to the federal government. What is one power of the federal government?

Know one of the following:

To print money

To declare war

To create an army

To make treaties

Bajo nuestra constitución, algunos poderes pertenecen al gobierno federal. ¿Cuál es un poder del gobierno federal?

Conozca una de las siguientes repuestas:

Pra imprimir el dinero

Para declarar guerra

Para crear a un ejército

Para hacer trados

42. Under our Constitution, some powers belong to the states. What is one
power of the states?

Provide schooling and education

Bajo nuestra constitución, algunos poderes pertenecen a los
estados. ¿Cuál es un poder de los estados?

Proporcionar suficiente educación

43. Who is the Governor of your state?

Answers will vary. Residents of the District of Columbia and U.S.
territories without a Governor should say "we don't have a Governor."

¿Quién es el gobernador de tu estado?

Las respuestas variarán. [Los residentes del distrito
de Columbia y de los territorios de los E.E.U.U. sin
un gobernador deben decir "no tenemos un
Gobernador."]

**See List of Representatives in back of book and write the answer
here:____**

44. What is the capital of your state?*

¿Cual es la capital de tu estado? *

Las respuestas variarán. Los residentes del distrito de
Columbia deben contestar a que la D.C. no es un

estado y no tienen una capital. Los residentes de los territorios de los E.E.U.U. deben nombrar la capital del territorio.

See List of Representatives in back of book and write the answer here:____

45. What are the two major political parties in the United States?*

Democratic and Republican

¿Cuáles son los dos partidos políticos principales en los Estados Unidos? *

Demócratas y Republicanos

46. What is the political party of the President now?

Democratic Party

¿Cuál es el partido político del presidente hoy?

Partido Demócrata

47. What is the name of the Speaker of the House of Representatives now?

Kevin McCarthy

¿Cuál es el nombre del Orador de la Cámara de Representantes hoy?

Kevin McCarthy

C: Rights and Responsibilities

Los derechos y responsabilidades

48. There are four amendments to the Constitution about who can vote. Describe one of them.

> Citizens eighteen (18) and older can vote.

> Any citizen can vote. (Women and men can vote.)

>> Hay cuatro enmiendas a la constitución sobre quién puede votar. Describa una de ellas.

>>> Ciudadanos de 18 años o mas puede votar.

>>> Cualquier ciudadano puede votar. (Las mujeres y los hombres pueden votar.)

49. What is one responsibility that is only for United States citizens?*

> Serve on a jury

>> ¿Cuál es una responsabilidad que tiene un ciudadano de los Estados Unidos? *

>> Servir en un jurado

50. What are two rights only for United States citizens?

> Apply for a federal job

> vote

>> ¿Cuáles son los derechos solamente para los ciudadanos de Estados Unidos?

>> Solicitar un trabajo federal

Votar

51. What are two rights of everyone living in the United States?

Freedom of expression

Freedom of speech

¿Cuáles son los derechos de cada uno que vive en los Estados Unidos?

Libertad de expresión

Libertad de hablar

52. What do we show loyalty to when we say the Pledge of Allegiance?

The United States and the flag

¿A Qué demostramos lealtad cuando hacemos la jura de la bandera?

A los Estados Unidos y la bandera

53. What is one promise you make when you become a United States citizen?

Defend the Constitution and laws of the United States

¿Cuál es la promesa que haces cuando tú te haces un ciudadano de Estados Unidos?

Defender la constitución y las leyes de los Estados Unidos

54. How old do citizens have to be to vote?*

Eighteen (18) and older

¿ Cual es la edad de un ciudadano para votar? *

Dieciocho (18) años y más

55. What are two ways that Americans can participate in their democracy?

Vote

Join a political party

¿Cuáles son dos maneras que los americanos pueden participar en su democracia?

Votar

Ensamblar un partido político

56. When is the last day you can send in federal income tax forms?*

April 15

¿Cuándo es el ultimo día que tú puedes enviar las formulas de impuesto federal? *

15 de abril

57. When must all men register for the Selective Service?

Between eighteen (18) and twenty-six (26)

¿Cuándo deben registrarse todos los hombres para el servicio selectivo?

Entre dieciocho (18) y veintiséis (26) años

AMERICAN HISTORY / HISTORIA AMERICANA

A: Colonial Period and Independence

Período e independencia coloniales

58. What is one reason colonists came to America?

Freedom

Political liberty

¿ Cuál es una razón que los colonizadores vinieron a América?

Libertad

Libertad política

59. Who lived in America before the Europeans arrived?

Native Americans

American Indians

¿Quién vivió en América antes de que llegaran los europeos?

Nativos americanos

Indios americanos

60. What group of people was taken to America and sold as slaves?

Africans

¿ Qué grupo de personas les vendieron en America como esclavos?

Africanos

61. Why did the colonists fight the British?

Because of high taxes (taxation without representation)

Because the British army stayed in their houses (boarding, quartering)

Because they didn't have self-government

¿Por qué los colonizadores lucharon con los Británicos?

Debido a los altos impuestos (impuestos sin la representación)

Porque el ejército británico permanecía en sus casas

(en guardia)

Porque no tenían gobierno autónomo

62. Who wrote the Declaration of Independence?

Thomas Jefferson

¿Quién escribió la Declaración de Independencia?

Thomas Jefferson

63. When was the Declaration of Independence adopted?

July 4, 1776

Cuándo fue adoptada la Declaración de Independencia?

De julio de 1776

64. There were 13 original states. Name three.

New York

New Jersey

Virgina

Había 13 estados originales. Nombre tres.

Nueva York

Nueva Jersey

Virginia

65. What happened at the Constitutional Convention?

The Constitution was written.

¿Qué sucedió en la convención constitucional?

La constitución fue escrita.

66. When was the Constitution written?

1787

¿Cuándo fue escrita la constitución?

1787

67. The Federalist Papers supported the passage of the U.S. Constitution. Name one of the writers.

James Madison

Los papeles federalistas apoyaron el paso de la constitución de los E.E.U.U. Nombre uno de los escritores.

James Madison

68. What is one thing Benjamin Franklin is famous for?

U.S. diplomat

¿Por que fue famoso Benjamin Franklin?

Fue diplomatico de los E.E.U.U.

69. Who is the "Father of Our Country"?

George Washington

Quién es el "¿Padre de nuestro pais"?

George Washington

70. Who was the first President?*

    George Washington

        ¿Quién fue el primer presidente? *

        George Washington

71. What territory did the United States buy from France in 1803?

    The Louisiana Territory

        ¿Qué territorio los Estados Unidos compro a Francia en 1803?

        El territorio de Luisiana

72. Name one war fought by the United States in the 1800s.

    Spanish-American War

        Nombre una guerra que los Estados Unidos combatió en los años 1800s.

        Guerra hispanoamericana

73. Name the U.S. war between the North and the South.

    The Civil War

        Nombre la guerra de los E.E.U.U. entre el norte y el sur.

        La guerra civil

74. Name one problem that led to the Civil War.

    Slavery

        Nombre un problema que llevó a la guerra civil.

        Esclavitud

75. What was one important thing that Abraham Lincoln did?*

Freed the slaves (Emancipation Proclamation)

¿Que cosa importante hizo Abraham Lincoln? *

Liberó los esclavos (la proclamación de la emancipación)

76. What did the Emancipation Proclamation do?

Freed the slaves

¿Qué hizo la proclamación de la emancipación?

Liberó los esclavos

77. What did Susan B. Anthony do?

Fought for women's rights

¿Qué hizo Susan B. Anthony?

Luchó por los derechos de las mujeres

Recent American History
and Other Important Historical Information

La reciente historia americana y otra importante

información histórica

78. Name one war fought by the United States in the 1900s.*

World War II

Nombre una guerra de los Estados Unidos en los años 1900s.*

Segunda Guerra Mundial

79. Who was President during World War I?

Woodrow Wilson

¿Quién fue presidente durante la Primera Guerra Mundial?

Woodrow Wilson

80. Who was President during the Great Depression and World War II?

Franklin Roosevelt

¿Quién fue presidente durante la Gran Depresión y la Segunda Guerra Mundial?

Franklin Roosevelt

81. Who did the United States fight in World War II?

Japan, Germany and Italy

¿Con quien peleo los Estados Unidos en la Segunda Guerra Mundial?

Japón, Alemania e Italia

82. Before he was President, Eisenhower was a general. What war was he in?

World War II

Antes que fuera presidente, Eisenhower era un general. ¿En qué guerra estubo él?

Segunda Guerra Mundial

83. During the Cold War, what was the main concern of the United States?

Communism

¿Durante la guerra fría, cuál era la mayor preocupación de los Estados Unidos?

Comunismo

84. What movement tried to end racial discrimination?

civil rights movement

¿Qué movimiento intentó terminar la discriminación racial?

Los derechos civiles (movimiento)

85. What did Martin Luther King, Jr. do?*

Fought for civil rights

¿Qué hizo Martin Luther King, Jr.? *

Luchó por los derechos civiles

86. What major event happened on September 11, 2001 in the United States?

Terrorists attacked the United States.

¿Qué gran evento sucedió el 11 de septiembre de 2001 en los Estados Unidos?

Los terroristas atacaron los Estados Unidos.

87. Name one American Indian tribe in the United States.

Cherokee

Navajo

Apache

Nombre una tribu india americana en los Estados Unidos.

Cherokee

Navajo

Apache

[Adjudicators will be supplied with a complete list.][Suministrarán una lista completa.]

INTEGRATED CIVICS / CÍVIC INTEGRADO

Geography /.Geografía

88. Name one of the two longest rivers in the United States.

Missouri or Mississippi river

Nombre uno de los dos ríos más largos en los Estados Unidos.

Rio Missouri o Mississippi

89. What ocean is on the West Coast of the United States?

Pacific Ocean

¿Qué océano está en la costa oeste de los Estados Unidos?

Pacífico

90. What ocean is on the East Coast of the United States?

Atlantic Ocean

¿Qué océano está en la costa este de los Estados Unidos?

Atlántico (océano)

91. Name one U.S. territory.

Puerto Rico

Nombre un territorio de los E.E.U.U..

Puerto Rico

92. Name one state that borders Canada.

New York

Nombre un estado fronterizo con Canadá.

Nueva York

93. Name one state that borders Mexico.

California

Nombre un estado fronterizo con México

California

94. What is the capital of the United States?*

Washington, D.C.

¿Cual ciudad es la capital de los Estados Unidos? *

Washington, D.C.

95. Where is the Statue of Liberty?*

New York Harbor

¿Dónde está la estatua de la libertad? *

En el puerto de Nueva York

Symbols / Símbolos

96. Why does the flag have 13 stripes?

Because there were 13 original colonies

¿Por qué la bandera tiene 13 rayas?

Porque había 13 colonias originales

97. Why does the flag have 50 stars?*

Because there is one star for each state

¿Por qué la bandera tiene 50 estrellas? *

Porque hay una estrella por cada estado

98. What is the name of the national anthem?

The Star-Spangled Banner

¿Cuál es el nombre del himno nacional?

The Star-Spangled Banner

Holidays./.Días de fiesta

99. When do we celebrate Independence Day?*

    July 4

        ¿Cuándo celebramos Día de la Independencia? *

        4 de Julio

100. Name two national U.S. holidays.

    Independence Day

    Christmas

        Nombre dos días de fiesta nacionales de los E.E.U.U.

        Día de la independencia

        La Navidad

Sample Written Sentences

You will be asked to write a sample sentence. Normally you can make up
to three (3) errors in writing and still pass the test.
Be careful to listen to each word the examiner reads. Make sure to write
each word, even if you think it is not needed grammatically, if the
examiner reads a word; please write out every word that is dictated.

1) A senator is elected for 6 years.

2) Kamala Harris is the Vice President of the United States.

3) All people want to be free.

4) America is the land of freedom.

5) All American citizens have the right to vote.

6) America is the home of the brave.

7) America is the land of the free.

8) Joseph Biden is the President of the United States.

9) Citizens have the right to vote.

10) Congress is part of the American government.

11) Congress meets in Washington DC.

12) Congress passes laws in the United States.

13) George Washington was the first president.

14) I want to be a citizen of the United States.

15) I want to be an American citizen.

16) I want to become an American so I can vote.

17) It is important for all citizens to vote.

18) Many people come to America for freedom.

19) Many people have died for freedom.

20) Martha Washington was the first lady.

21) Only Congress can declare war.

22) Our Government is divided into three branches.

23) People in America have the right to freedom.

24) People vote for the President in November.

25) The American flag has stars and stripes.

26) The American flag has 13 stripes.

27) The capital of the United States is Washington DC.

28) The colors of the flag are red white and blue.

29) The Constitution is the supreme law of our land.

30) The flag of the United States has 50 stars.

31) The House and Senate are parts of Congress

32) The President enforces the laws.

33) The President has the power of veto.

34) The President is elected every 4 years.

35) The President lives in the White House.

36) The President lives in Washington D.C.

37) The President must be an American citizen.

38) The President must be born in the United States.

39) The President signs bills into law.

40) The stars of the American flag are white.

41) The White House is in Washington, DC.

42) The United States flag is red white and blue.

43) The United States of America has 50 states.

List of Representatives and Capitals

Members of the Senate

Representatives are subject to change.

Find your state to identify your two Senators

Source: http://Senate.gov Updated January 2023

What is a class? - Article I, section 3 of the Constitution requires the Senate to be divided into three classes for purposes of elections. Senators are elected to six-year terms, and every two years the members of one class—approximately one-third of the senators—face election or reelection. Terms for senators in Class I expire in 2019, Class II in 2021, and Class III in 2023.

U.S. State Postal Abbreviations List

Alabama – AL   Alaska – AK   Arizona – AZ   Arkansas - AR

California – CA   Colorado – CO   Connecticut - CT

Delaware – DE   District of Columbia - DC

Florida - FL

Georgia - GA

Hawaii - HI

Idaho – ID   Illinois – IL   Indiana – IN   Iowa - IA

Kansas – KS   Kentucky - KY

Louisiana - LA

Maine – ME   Maryland – MD   Massachusetts – MA   Michigan – MI   Minnesota – MN   Mississippi – MS   Missouri – MO Montana - MT

Nebraska – NE   Nevada – NV   New Hampshire – NH   New Jersey – NJ   New Mexico – NM   New York – NY   North Carolina – NC   North Dakota - ND

Ohio – OH   Oklahoma – OK   Oregon - OR

Pennsylvania - PA

Rhode Island - RI

South Carolina – SC   South Dakota - SD

Tennessee – TN   Texas - TX

Utah - UT

Vermont – VT   Virginia - VA

Washington – WA   West Virginia – WV   Wisconsin – WI Wyoming - WY

US Commonwealth and Territories

American Samoa – AS   Federated States of Micronesia – FM   Guam – GU   Marshall Islands - MH

Northern Mariana Islands – MP   Palau – PW   Puerto Rico – PR Virgin Islands

# Senators of the 118th Congress
D= Democratic   R= Republican

Source: https://en.wikipedia.org/wiki/118th_United_States_Congress

D= Democratic   R= Republican

Source: https://www.senate.gov/senators/index.htm

Class - Article I, section 3 of the Constitution requires the Senate to be divided into three classes for purposes of elections. Senators are elected to six-year terms, and every two years the members of one class—approximately one-third of the senators—face election or reelection.

Tommy Tuberville	Republican	Alabama
Katie Britt	Republican	Alabama
Lisa Murkowski	Republican	Alaska
Dan Sullivan	Republican	Alaska
Kyrsten Sinema	Democratic	Arizona
Mark Kelly	Democratic	Arizona
John Boozman	Republican	Arkansas
Tom Cotton	Republican	Arkansas
Dianne Feinstein	Democratic	California
Alex Padilla	Democratic	California
Michael Bennet	Democratic	Colorado
John Hickenlooper	Democratic	Colorado
Richard Blumenthal	Democratic	Connecticut
Chris Murphy	Democratic	Connecticut
Tom Carper	Democratic	Delaware
Chris Coons	Democratic	Delaware
Marco Rubio	Republican	Florida
Rick Scott	Republican	Florida
Jon Ossoff	Democratic	Georgia
Brian Schatz	Democratic	Hawaii
Mazie Hirono	Democratic	Hawaii
Mike Crapo	Republican	Idaho
Jim Risch	Republican	Idaho

Dick Durbin	Democratic	Illinois
Tammy Duckworth	Democratic	Illinois
Todd Young	Republican	Indiana
Mike Braun	Republican	Indiana
Chuck Grassley	Republican	Iowa
Joni Ernst	Republican	Iowa
Jerry Moran	Republican	Kansas
Roger Marshall	Republican	Kansas
Mitch McConnell	Republican	Kentucky
Rand Paul	Republican	Kentucky
Bill Cassidy	Republican	Louisiana
John Neely Kennedy	Republican	Louisiana
Susan Collins	Republican	Maine
Angus King	Independent	Maine
Ben Cardin	Democratic	Maryland
Chris Van Hollen	Democratic	Maryland
Elizabeth Warren	Democratic	Massachusetts
Ed Markey	Democratic	Massachusetts
Debbie Stabenow	Democratic	Michigan
Gary Peters	Democratic	Michigan
Amy Klobuchar	Democratic	Minnesota
Tina Smith	Democratic	Minnesota
Roger Wicker	Republican	Mississippi
Cindy Hyde-Smith	Republican	Mississippi
Josh Hawley	Republican	Missouri
Eric Schmitt	Republican	Missouri
Jon Tester	Democratic	Montana
Steve Daines	Republican	Montana
Deb Fischer	Republican	Nebraska
Ben Sasse	Republican	Nebraska
TBD	Republican	Nebraska
Catherine Cortez Masto	Democratic	Nevada
Jacky Rosen	Democratic	Nevada
Jeanne Shaheen	Democratic	New Hampshire

Maggie Hassan	Democratic	New Hampshire
Bob Menendez	Democratic	New Jersey
Cory Booker	Democratic	New Jersey
Martin Heinrich	Democratic	New Mexico
Ben Ray Luján	Democratic	New Mexico
Chuck Schumer	Democratic	New York
Kirsten Gillibrand	Democratic	New York
Thom Tillis	Republican	North Carolina
Ted Budd *	Republican	North Carolina
John Hoeven	Republican	North Dakota
Kevin Cramer	Republican	North Dakota
Sherrod Brown	Democratic	Ohio
J. D. Vance *	Republican	Ohio
James Lankford	Republican	Oklahoma
Markwayne Mullin *	Republican	Oklahoma
Ron Wyden	Democratic	Oregon
Jeff Merkley	Democratic	Oregon
Bob Casey, Jr.	Democratic	Pennsylvania
John Fetterman	Democratic	Pennsylvania
Jack Reed	Democratic	Rhode Island
Sheldon Whitehouse	Democratic	Rhode Island
Lindsey Graham	Republican	South Carolina
Tim Scott	Republican	South Carolina
John Thune	Republican	South Dakota
Mike Rounds	Republican	South Dakota
Marsha Blackburn	Republican	Tennessee
Bill Hagerty	Republican	Tennessee
John Cornyn	Republican	Texas
Ted Cruz	Republican	Texas
Mike Lee	Republican	Utah
Mitt Romney	Republican	Utah
Bernie Sanders	Independent	Vermont

Peter Welch	Democratic	Vermont
Mark Warner	Democratic	Virginia
Tim Kaine	Democratic	Virginia
Patty Murray	Democratic	Washington
Maria Cantwell	Democratic	Washington
Joe Manchin	Democratic	West Virginia
Shelley Moore Capito	Republican	West Virginia
Ron Johnson	Republican	Wisconsin
Tammy Baldwin	Democratic	Wisconsin
John Barrasso	Republican	Wyoming
Cynthia Lummis	Republican	Wyoming

List of State Governors

Governors are subject to change. District of Columbia residents should answer that D.C. is not a state and does not have a capital. Residents of U.S. territories should name the capital of the territory.

Source:
https://en.wikipedia.org/wiki/List_of_current_United_States_governors

*Denotes newly elected Governors

*Denotes newly elected Governors 2022

Alabama – Kay Ivey

Alaska – Mike Dunaway

Arizona – To be determined

Arkansas – Asa Hutchinson.

California – Gavin Newsom

Colorado – Jared Polis

Connecticut – Ned Lamont

Delaware – John Carney

Florida – Ron DeSantis

Georgia – Brian Kemp

Hawaii – David Ige

Idaho – Brad Little

Illinois – J.B. Pritzker

Indiana – Eric Holcomb

Iowa – Kim Reynolds

Kansas – Laura Kelly

Kentucky – Andy Beshear

Louisiana – John Bel Edwards

Maine – Janet Mills

Maryland – Larry Hogan

Massachusetts – Charlie Baker

Michigan – Gretchen Whitmer

Minnesota – Tim Walz

Mississippi – Tate Reeves

Missouri – Mike Parson

Montana – Greg Gianforte*

Nebraska – Jim Pillen

Nevada – Steve Sisolak

New Hampshire – Chris Sununu

New Jersey – Phil Murphy

New Mexico – Michelle Lujan Grisham

New York – Kathy Hochul

North Carolina – Ray Cooper

North Dakota – Doug Burgum

Ohio – Mike DeWine

Oklahoma – Kevin Stitt

Oregon – Tina Kotek

Pennsylvania – Josh Shapiro

Rhode Island – Daniel McKee

South Carolina – Henri McMaster

South Dakota – Kristi Noem

Tennessee – Bill Lee

Texas – Greg Abbott

Utah – Spencer Cox

Vermont – Phil Scott

Virginia – Glenn Youngkin

Washington – Jay Inslee

West Virginia – Jim Justice

Wisconsin – Tony Evers

Wyoming – Mark Gordon

List of State Capitals

Alabama - Montgomery

Alaska - Juneau

Arizona - Phoenix

Arkansas - Little Rock

California - Sacramento

Colorado - Denver

Connecticut - Hartford

Delaware - Dover

Florida - Tallahassee

Georgia - Atlanta

Hawaii - Honolulu

Idaho - Boise

Illinois - Springfield

Indiana - Indianapolis

Iowa - Des Moines

Kansas - Topeka

Kentucky - Frankfort

Louisiana - Baton Rouge

Maine - Augusta

Maryland - Annapolis

Massachusetts - Boston

Michigan - Lansing

Minnesota - St. Paul

Mississippi - Jackson

Missouri - Jefferson City

Montana - Helena

Nebraska - Lincoln

Nevada - Carson City

New Hampshire - Concord

New Jersey - Trenton

New Mexico - Santa Fe

New York - Albany

North Carolina - Raleigh

North Dakota - Bismarck

Ohio - Columbus

Oklahoma - Oklahoma City

Oregon - Salem

Pennsylvania - Harrisburg

Rhode Island - Providence

South Carolina - Columbia

South Dakota - Pierre

Tennessee - Nashville

Texas - Austin

Utah - Salt Lake City

Vermont - Montpelier

Virginia - Richmond

Washington - Olympia

West Virginia - Charleston

Wisconsin - Madison

Wyoming – Cheyenne

Avoid Scams

From the USCIS website: http://www.uscis.gov/avoidscams

The wrong help can hurt

Are you getting the right immigration help?

Many people offer help with immigration services. Unfortunately, not all are authorized to do so. While many of these unauthorized practitioners mean well, all too many of them are out to rip you off. This is against the law and may be considered an immigration services scam.

If you need help filing an application or petition with USCIS, be sure to seek assistance from the right place, and from people that are authorized to help. Going to the wrong place can:

Delay your application or petition

Cost you unnecessary fees

Possibly lead to removal proceedings

This site can help you avoid immigration services scams. Remember: Know the facts when it comes to immigration assistance, because the Wrong Help Can Hurt.

Tools to Help You Avoid Scammers

USCIS wants to combat immigration services scams by equipping applicants, legal service providers and community-based organizations with the knowledge and tools they need to detect and protect themselves from dishonest practices.

To accomplish this goal, USCIS launched the Unauthorized Practice of Immigration Law (UPIL) Initiative. As part of the effort, we've partnered with several government agencies to identify resources that can help you avoid immigration services scams.

Empower yourself by using our online educational resources, which include:

The top things to know before and after filing an application or petition

A list of common immigration services scams

State-by-state information on where you can report an immigration services scam

Advice on finding authorized legal help

Information on becoming an authorized legal immigration service provider

Educational tools you can print and share

This page can be found at: http://www.uscis.gov/avoidscams.

ABOUT THE AUTHOR

Mike Swedenberg saw a need to assemble a study guide to help those persons wishing to immigrate to the United States whose second language is English. This study guide is annotated with the names of current Representatives that all applicants must know. The list is current for State Governors, US Senators and US Congressmen. This list will be updated at each election cycle.

Other books by the Author
The Road Warrior a sales manual
Advertising Copywriting and the Unique Selling Proposition
Smart Money Stupid Money – Advice
21 ½ Things to Know Before You Self Publish – Advice
How to Publish an eBook - Advice

www.ingramcontent.com/pod-product-compliance
Lightning Source LLC
Chambersburg PA
CBHW051353150726
48000CB00003B/1162